Purnell
£3.25
U.K. only

British Library Cataloguing in Publication Data
Dukes of Hazzard annual.—1986
1. Anthologies
082 AC5

ISBN 0 361 06774 7

Published 1985 by Purnell Books, Paulton, Bristol BS18 5LQ,
a member of the BPCC group
Phototypeset by Quadraset Limited
Made and Printed in Italy

THE DUKES OF HAZZARD™ ANNUAL

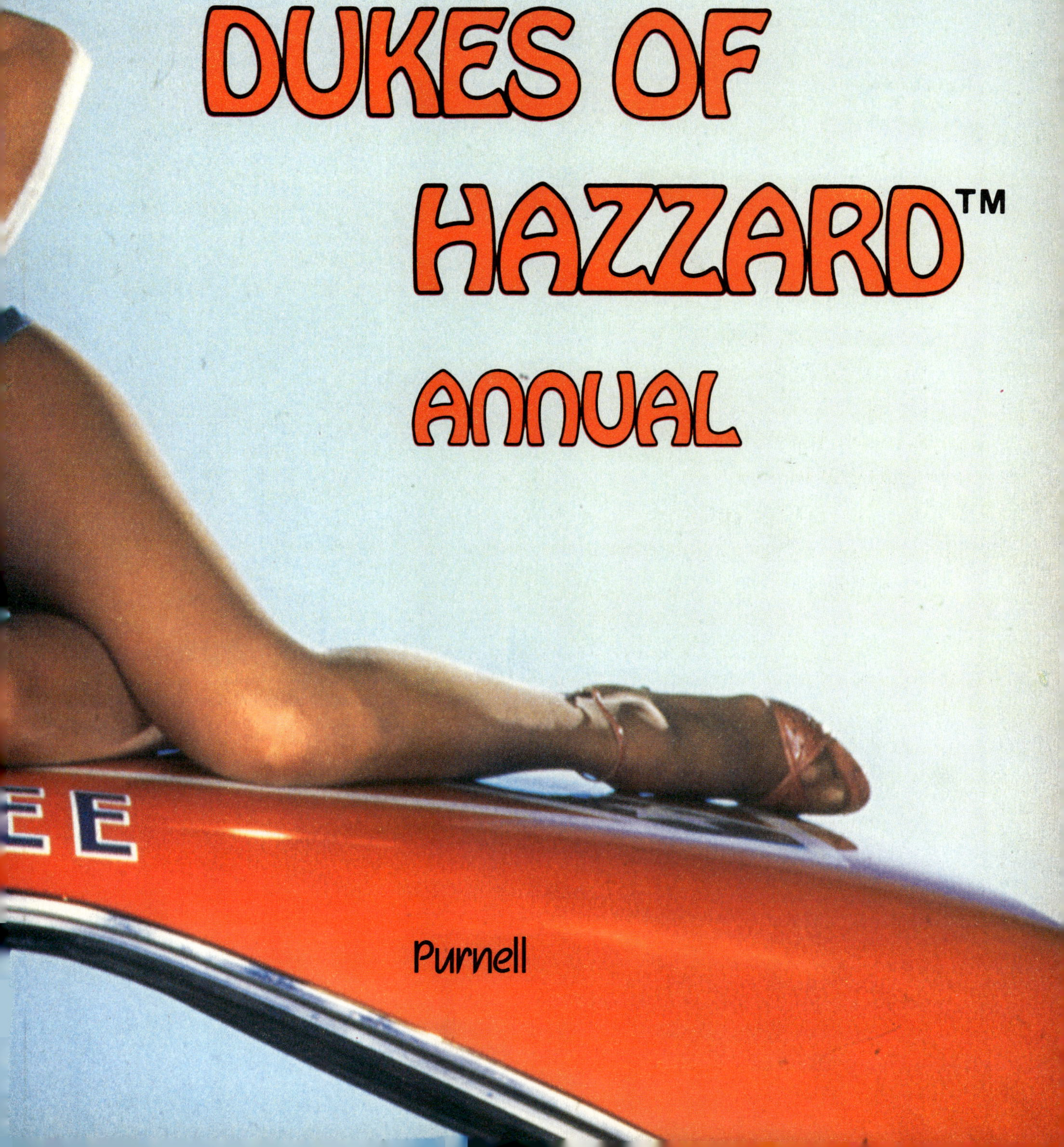

Purnell

A Flash

When you've as much money as Boss Hogg, you have to realise there's other folks around who'd like to help you spend it . . .

"When I catch them lousy, low-down, good-for-nothings, I'll . . . I'll . . ."

Mutterings and mumblings of this sort had been emanating from Boss's office for most of the morning, ever since Boss had come in to work, and found that his private and personal safe had been opened in the night — and not by anyone wanting to put anything *in*!

Enos and Rosco weren't paying him much attention, though. They had other things on their minds. Flash had stayed in the office overnight — as she sometimes did if she was already asleep when it came time for them to lock up — but this morning she was nowhere to be seen.

Enos had put down a bowl of her favourite food for her breakfast, but apparently not even the delicious aroma of that was tempting her back from wherever she'd gone.

"She must be miles away," said Rosco, looking worried. "She can smell that grub from right over the other side of town."

"I know," agreed Enos, miserably. "You thinkin' what I'm thinkin', buddy?"

"Reckon I am," nodded Rosco. "Reckon we're both thinkin' that the guys who took Boss's money also took the witness to their crime."

"If they've harmed her . . ." began Enos, through gritted teeth.

"Don't worry, pal," said Rosco, sounding more cheerful and confident than he felt. "They probably just put her in their car so's she wouldn't raise the alarm by barking. They'll set her free somewhere outside town an' someone will recognise her."

"Gee, I sure hope you're right," said Enos . . .

Boss's favourite piece of office furniture.

# of Inspiration

Meanwhile, out on Highway 9, Bo and Luke had been doing some early morning deliveries for Uncle Jesse. They stopped at a roadside diner for a cup of coffee, and as they went in . . .

"There goes Boss Hogg," said Bo, surprised to see a familiar white Cadillac pass by the diner at such an early hour.

"No, it ain't," Bo corrected himself. "Those aren't Boss's plates. It's just like his car, though, only cleaner."

"Come on, cuz," Luke interrupted him. "Let's go get that coffee."

And the two boys went inside, forgetting all about the white car.

Enos and Rosco, they didn't get much work done that morning, what with the robbery, an' Flash's disappearance, an' all. Boss had them in his office looking for clues for round about an hour mid-morning, an' when they came out . . .

"Flash!" Rosco and Enos cried out in unison at the sight of their beloved Flash, calmly eating out of her bowl, and looking as though she hadn't a care in the world.

She did look a bit bedraggled though, and she seemed rather tired, as though she had walked quite a long way. Rosco and Enos were convinced that their theory had been right — Flash had been taken by the safe-robbers, and released to find her own way home.

"Just you wait till we catch up with them, Flash old girl," said Enos, bending down to pick her up and hug her close. "Ain't no one gonna take you away from us again. No sirree."

Just at that moment Boss

"Honey, I couldn't live without ya!"

appeared in his office doorway, and even though he isn't exactly known as the most warm-hearted of guys, even he had to admit that he was pleased to see their faithful friend back home again.

"Tell you what, Rosco," he said, in a rare mood of generosity, "you can buy her that dog food that's a coupla cents dearer this week."

He turned to go back into his office, pausing just long enough to add, more characteristically:

"Just for this week, mind."

"What's that you say?"

You've heard all that stuff about pets who try to tell their owners things . . .? Well, Rosco always reckoned that folks were just makin' those stories up. But right now he wasn't quite so sure . . .

"What is it, girl?" said Rosco, later that afternoon, when Flash nuzzled up to his ear for what must have been the twentieth time. "If only I could speak your language."

He turned to Enos: "I'm sure she's trying to tell me something, but there ain't no way I can figure out what it is. Any ideas?"

Enos was as puzzled as Rosco.

"Could be she's trying to give us a clue about them there safe-

"Now, who on earth was **that**?"

robbers," he guessed. "But I sure don't know as how we're gonna be able to figure it out!"

Flash went home with Rosco to her comfortable kennel that evening, and Rosco hoped she'd just settle down for a good night's sleep — sleeping being one of her favourite pastimes — and wake up in the morning feeling quite her old self again.

But something very odd happened . . .

Boss Hogg had forgotten to go over some urgent business with Rosco at the office, and he stopped by Rosco's place on his way home. He turned into Rosco's driveway, and saw Flash sitting quietly outside her kennel. Then Flash saw him . . .

Well, Flash just went wild! No one had ever seen her so excited before. She barked and howled, and ran backwards and forwards, snapping furiously in the direction of Boss's white Cadillac.

Rosco came running out to find out whatever was going on, and the two of them tried to calm her down. But it was only when Boss reversed the Cadillac down the drive and parked it round the corner out of sight that Flash finally stopped barking and became once more her old, placid self.

"Well, whaddya make of that?" said Rosco, when Boss returned. He was astonished at Flash's crazy behaviour.

"I sure don't know," replied the flustered Boss. "But if she pulls any more tricks like that one she can forget that fancy dog food. How much is a pound of scraps?"

The two of them went inside the house to get on with the office work, and pretty soon the incident had faded from their minds. They couldn't see any reason for Flash's outburst, so they hardly gave it another thought.

"No more o' that fancy dog food for her!"

Which just goes to show how good they both were at lookin' for clues . . . Anyway, come the following lunch break, Rosco and Enos were out on patrol. They stopped off at that selfsame diner which the Duke boys had been in the day before . . .

And which, as it happened, they were in again.

"Remind me to book 'em for something before we leave," said Rosco to Enos when the boys gave them a wave and a 'Howdy, fellas' from a neighbouring table.

Rosco and Enos settled down to their cheeseburgers, and Rosco started to tell his deputy what had happened the previous evening, when Boss had called at his place.

Enos didn't know what to

make of it either.

So it was lucky really, that the Duke boys overheard . . .

They'd heard all about the safe-breaking incident from the talk in the Boar's Nest the night before, and they knew that the robbers had taken Flash with them in their car.

It didn't take them long to figure out that Flash must have been trying to give Rosco and Boss a clue about what kind of car it was she'd been in. It must've been a white Cadillac, and since Boss was hardly likely to rob himself — yes, there were some things even *he* wouldn't stoop to — then it must've been someone else with a white Cadillac, just like his.

"That rings a bell," said Bo, thinking hard. "Yeah, I remember now! We saw a white Cadillac just like Boss's yesterday. Now where was it . . .?"

"It was right outside here," Luke finished off for him, and Bo nodded excitedly: "That's right! And it was headed west down the highway towards those old mine workings at Rockabilly Ridge."

Just at that moment the waitress arrived with their order. They looked at the waitress, then they looked at each other. "Sorry, we'll have to take a rain check," said Bo, piling a handful of coins onto the table.

"We just gotta go," said Luke, as they headed for the door.

"Wonder what's got into them?" said Enos, as the door swung closed behind them and almost immediately there came the sound of the General's engine bursting into action.

Whilst Enos and Rosco got busy eatin', Bo 'n' Luke got busy drivin' . . .

"Say, cuz," began Bo, thoughtfully, "strikes me maybe we've been a bit too quick off the mark here. After all, we haven't got much to go on. You can't just go round accusin' folks of stealing just because they drive white Cadillacs."

"Yeah, I've been thinking about that," replied Luke. "But I reckon there must be something suspicious about these guys. After all, you and I know all the smart cars in Hazzard, an' if these guys were visiting someone we'd have heard about it in the Boar's Nest. You don't keep much to yourself in Hazzard."

Bo grinned. "You're right, cuz," he agreed.

As it turned out, the boys didn't need any more convincing that they had the right guys when they neared the old mines at Rockabilly Ridge.

Bo 'n' Luke know every dirt track in Hazzard like the backs of their hands, and it didn't take them long to explore some of the most isolated roads round the mines. Pretty soon they spotted the Cadillac parked almost out of sight behind some boulders.

Now, the reason they didn't need convincing that they had found the safe-robbers was that the minute the two occupants of the Cadillac saw the General coming towards them they shot off with a screech of tyres to make their escape.

You won't need telling what happened next . . .

The General's engine burst into life.

The smartest chassis in town.

"Is it all here?"

There was the kind of car chase you only ever see in the movies — or in Hazzard County, if you ever visit. The white Cadillac was a strong, powerful car, and there were times when it looked like it might get away.

But the General wasn't about to be beaten by no pretty face, and he put on an extra surge or two at all the right moments, until at least, with a terrific *Yee-Haaa!* from the Dukes, the General hurtled past the Cadillac on a straight stretch of road, and brought it to a defeated halt.

It was just all 'happy ending' kinda stuff after that . . .

The Duke boys delivered the safe-robbers into the hands of Rosco and Enos, who had been munching away contentedly in the diner whilst all the excitement had been going on.

A search of the old mine workings revealed Boss's stolen property, plus a great deal more from various break-ins which had been reported in Hazzard recently.

Flash became quite a local celebrity, and the story of how she gave the vital clue which caught the criminals was front page news in the Hazzard papers for a week. (Yeah, well, not too much happens in Hazzard, you know . . .)

All the folks who'd had property returned safely to them wanted to thank whoever was responsible for finding it. The Duke boys wouldn't have taken any rewards, of course, but in actual fact whether they would or wouldn't didn't become an issue. Nope, the rewards weren't offered to them . . .

Flash was the one who got the rewards — bag after bag of big, juicy bones, box after box of dog food, and packet after packet of dog biscuits.

Boss surveyed the pile of stuff on his office floor. "Flash'll never eat all that in years," he moaned to Rosco and Enos. Then a thought struck him: "Wonder if I could set up a pet food stall in one of them there cells . . ."

"This place is full of crooks . . ."

Hazzard Howlers

Radio announcer: "Here is an urgent message for all drivers travelling to Cincinatti on Route 59 . . . Route 59 doesn't go to Cincinatti."

What do you get if you cross a sheep with a pool table?
Baa-billiards.

What sort of fur should you get from a skunk?
As fur as possible.

Rosco: "There's a man at the door with a funny face."
Boss: "Tell him you've already got one."

Enos and Rosco were waiting outside a baseball game.
Enos: "Gee, I wish I'd bought along the kitchen dresser."
Rosco: "Whatever for?"
Enos: "I left the tickets on it."

Rosco: "I've lost my dog. I'd like to put an ad in your paper."
Editor: "Why, can your dog read?"

Texas farmer: "Nice place you got here. How big?"
Uncle Jesse: "Well, I reckon we got an acre or two."
Texas farmer: "Huh. I've got a place that takes me a week to drive round. What do you say to that?"
Uncle Jesse: "I say it's time you got yourself a new car."

Rosco: "Look out the window. See if our new blinker light is working."
Enos: "Yes . . . No . . . Yes . . . No . . . Yes . . ."

Dentist: "That's the biggest cavity I've ever seen . . . ever seen . . . ever seen . . ."
Cooter: "There's no need to repeat yourself."
Dentist: "I didn't. That was the echo."

Cowboy: "Hi there. My name's Tex."
Daisy: "Oh, so you're from Texas?"
Cowboy: "Nope. Louisiana."
Daisy: "Then why do you call yourself Tex?"
Cowboy: "It sounds better than Louise."

What do you get if you cross an alarm clock with a whoopee cushion?
A rude awakening.

Bo: "What sits on top of a hill at night, howls at the moon, and is made of cement?"
Luke: "I give up. What is it?"
Bo: "A coyote."
Luke: "But what about the cement?"
Bo: "I just threw that in to make it hard."

Fit

Seems like it ain't just in sunny California folks've gone fitness mad. Even in Hazzard these days there's always someone wantin' to tell you that this thing here's real good for you, an' this other thing here ain't. Ol' Luke, he got bitten by that whole health and fitness bug . . .

"Want some blueberry pie, Luke?" asked Daisy, dishing out generous helpings for Bo and Uncle Jesse, who tucked in enthusiastically.

But Luke just smiled indulgently and covered his plate. "No thanks, Daisy," he said, looking smug, like a person who knows something other people don't. "Guess I'm the only one here who understands that all that starch and sugar and stuff is real bad for you. Yes sirree, real bad."

"Real dee-licious though, ain't it?" murmured Bo, through a mouthful of pie. "Any more going, Daisy?"

Luke had been fussy about his food for a week or two now, and the Dukes were just beginning to realise that he really was serious about all this sensible eating. He'd started going into the health food store in town, and coming out with appetising-looking stuff like garlic crackers and spinach-flavoured yoghurt . . .

And this new fitness craze didn't just stop at a change in his diet . . .

Every morning he was up at the crack of dawn — instead of setting an alarm clock he just moved the cockerel's favourite perch to right outside his bedroom window — and went off jogging, for mile after mile around Hazzard County, while everyone else was still dreaming!

He'd come back hours later, take a shower, and tuck into a dried apricot or two whilst the others helped themselves to eggs, and toast, and maple syrup pancakes, and lots of lovely, fresh-brewed coffee. (Luke would have a glass of water — with maybe a slice of lemon for added flavour.)

When he heard one day that a crack unit of the US Marines were coming to Hazzard to give demonstrations — and that the public could try out their assault course — Luke could hardly wait till they arrived. He'd heard tell you had to be real fit to handle that assault course . . .

You sure did . . . and one by

for a DUKE

one all the young guys in Hazzard who tried it out only got as far as the first few obstacles.

Then came Luke's turn, and the new superfit version hurtled over the entire course in terrific style — swinging through the air on ropes, clambering up nets and walls, crawling through narrow pipes, and finally hurtling over a precariously balanced ropebridge.

Luke's performance on the assault course earned him a cheer from the watching Marines, and they were keen to sign him up for a tour of duty. For a moment, Luke was tempted, but when he thought about it real hard he knew he'd miss the family and the farm far too much.

'Course, no one knew then, but as it turned out a much more dramatic 'assault course' lay just round life's next corner for Luke. Yes sir, an' this one was gonna be the real McCoy . . .

"Hey, cuz, what's that smoke back there?" queried Bo, looking in his driver's mirror as

Looks in pretty good shape already, don't he?

"Where's that smoke comin' from, Bo?"

the two boys drove outa town in the General. Luke turned round to get a better look, as Bo pulled over.

The boys got out and stood by the General, staring in concern into the distance, where they could see great billows of smoke rising into the sky. It seemed to be rising right over a built-up part of Hazzard . . .

"Let's get back there!" cried Luke, and the two of them leapt back into the General and sped off towards town.

"Could just be someone burning some rubbish," suggested Bo, trying to look on the bright side; but both boys were really worried by what they'd seen.

And rightly too, as it turned out, because as soon as they got back to town their worst suspicions were confirmed. There was a fire, and what's more it seemed to be . . .

"Oh no," whispered Luke,

"Oh no . . ."

hardly able to believe what he saw. "Rhuebottom's store is on fire!"

The boys ran to join the small group of horrified passers-by who had gathered outside the store. Someone told them that the fire had started in some garbage cartons stacked up outside, and was only just spreading to the shopfront. With a bit of luck it wouldn't have done too much damage by the time the fire brigade arrived, back from answering another call on the other side of town.

But sometimes things ain't as simple as they seem . . .

"Look!" cried a voice from the crowd. "Look over yonder! Mr Rhuebottom's trapped inside!"

All eyes turned in the direction the man was pointing. Sure enough, they were appalled to see Mr Rhuebottom waving frantically from a window which was in the direct line of the fire. He wasn't in real danger of being hurt at the moment, but if much more time went by things would start looking real tricky for him.

"Let's hope that ol' engine gets here soon," said another voice. "Ain't no way we're gonna be able to rescue him ourselves."

"Don't be too sure about that," murmured Luke, who was darting backwards and forwards, checking out the extent of the fire, and apparently planning something.

"Sure hope your partner ain't plannin' to try any crazy stunts," said someone to Bo.

As soon as the man spoke Bo realised what Luke was up to, and he spun round to stop his cousin trying out such a foolhardy plan. But it was too late . . .

"**Yeee-haaaa!**" Luke set off like an Olympic sprinter, hurtling forwards towards the flames, where they weren't too high. He leapt them with a terrific bound, like one of those Kung Fu movie stars. His fitness drive had sure come in handy!

A loud cheer went up from the crowd as they saw him reach the safety of part of the building which wasn't touched by the fire.

Moments later, he reappeared from round the back of the store

"Luke, don't . . ."

A hungry hero.

with a dazed Mr Rhuebottom. The poor storekeeper had panicked at the sight of the flames, and it was only when Luke appeared, and managed to calm him down, that he had been able to think out an escape route, through the back of the shop and his delivery yard.

It was only five minutes more before the fire brigade arrived, and in no time they had the fire under control. There would be quite a lot of repair work to do on the store, but, more important, Mr Rhuebottom had escaped injury.

As you can imagine, Luke was surrounded by folks patting him on the back and wanting to shake his hand.

But the boys thought Mr Rhuebottom looked very shaken, and they didn't want to hang around at the scene of the fire too long. They took him home with them in the General, to stay the night.

"Time enough in the morning to sort things out, Mr Rhuebottom," said Bo. "I reckon you'll find there'll be plenty of folks wanting to lend a hand."

Back at the farm, the grateful storekeeper lost no time in telling Uncle Jesse and Daisy the whole story of Luke's terrific rescue operation. Then he told them again . . . And again . . .

That night at dinner, Luke had a mighty good appetite. Daisy smiled as she helped him to another baked potato, and said:

"Not having your carrot juice tonight, cuz?"

Luke grinned sheepishly.

"Nope. Not tonight. Reckon I might've been overdoing that health and fitness thing a bit lately. Though I reckon I'll still try an' keep myself pretty fit. It paid dividends today."

"We'll drink to that," said the others, raising their glasses to the embarrassed hero, as he finished off his third helping.

Quickie Quiz

Can you answer these quick questions about the world of law enforcement? Remember, anything you say will be taken down . . .

1. One law enforcement agency in the USA is the FBI. What do the letters stand for?
2. Which fictional detective lived in Baker Street, London?
3. What is the name of the international organisation which helps many countries to track down criminals who have fled abroad?
4. What is the NYPD?
5. What is the CHP?
6. Where are police headquarters in London?
7. What is the name of Hazzard's sheriff?

Answers

1. Federal Bureau of Investigation, 2. Sherlock Holmes, 3. Interpol, 4. New York Police Department, 5. California Highway Patrol, 6. New Scotland Yard, 7. Rosco P. Coltrane.

Cross Country Chase

See who can be the first to cross Hazzard County — obeying all the instructions along the route. Throw a six to start and — if you want to make it really exasperating — one to finish, too!

Short cut — move forward 4 spaces
Out of gas — miss a turn
kdown — a turn
Wrong directions! — back 3 spaces
?
FINISH

King

You've heard the expression 'all's right with the world'? Well, you'd have had to tack the words 'except Cooter' onto the end of that old saying, one day last fall . . .

"Surely it can't be as bad as all that, Cooter?" asked Daisy, as she and the boys tried to cheer up their worried friend.

"Couldn't be much worse," replied Cooter miserably. "Here, you can see by my books. I've hardly done any business worth speaking of these two weeks past. Seems like all my old customers are takin' their business elsewhere."

"But why?" said Bo, voicing all their thoughts. "You're the best mechanic for miles around — everyone knows that."

"Seems everyone's forgotten then," was all Cooter could reply.

Daisy and the boys watched as poor old Cooter went sadly back to the garage. They decided they must find out what was going on — and fast.

As it happened it didn't take very long to find out the reason why all Cooter's old customers were taking their car repairs elsewhere. That night in the Boar's Nest, the place was buzzin' with talk about that very subject.

A typical snatch of the conversations the boys overheard went like this:

"An' I hear tell he attached the brake pedal to the throttle . . . Deke Daniels only found out when he tried to stop outside his garage . . ."

"So that's the reason!" said Bo. "Someone's been spreading rumours about Cooter's work not being up to scratch."

First thing the next morning Uncle Jesse and the boys arrived at Cooter's place to tell him they'd found out what was going on. But all they found was a sign saying 'Closed Today'.

"This is serious," said Luke. "Cooter mustn't have any work at all today. If it goes on much longer like this he'll be outa business."

"We gotta find out who's spreading these rumours," said Bo. "And we gotta put a stop to them, right now!"

Any guesses, you folks out there . . .?

Enos's naturally rather doleful expression had taken on another twenty degrees of dole that morning. "Well, I sure don't think it's right," he was saying to Rosco.

Carburettor

"Now what do we do?"

"What's that, deputy?" enquired his senior officer.

"I don't think it's right that Boss is spreading all these malicious rumours about Cooter's work," explained Enos. "People are startin' to believe them."

"I rather imagine that was the general idea," replied Rosco. "You know Boss wants to go into the garage business himself. How can he do that if there's already a real good mechanic in Hazzard, namely Cooter?"

"Yes, but . . ." began Enos.

Rosco looked at Enos sideways. "Deputy," he began, meaningfully. "Deputy Enos — you wanna remain a deputy for quite some time? Remember you'll need Boss's recommendation for promotion."

Enos might be a bit slow sometimes, but he caught on fast enough on this occasion. "Yeah, well," he finished off lamely, "I just think it's a bit mean, that's all."

You know that little voice that lives inside you and

"Yes, but . . ."

know, the winner takes the title 'King Carburettor'."

"That's right," said Luke, catching on fast. "We gotta make sure Cooter enters — he'll win it easy. Then folks'll know all these stories aren't true."

"Yeah, an' I can think of a way to make it work even better," said Bo. "Let's persuade Boss to enter, too. He's bound to make a hotch-potch of the whole thing. That'll be the end of his career in the garage business — before it even starts!"

keeps on whispering little messages every now and then? Some folks call it their conscience. Well, ol' Enos's conscience wasn't so much whispering as hollerin' out the message loud and clear . . .

". . . so I thought if I told you maybe you could do something about it."

Enos had decided he had to try to stop Boss putting Cooter out of business, and the only ones he could think of to confide in were the Dukes. He drove on out to the farm on his day off, and told them all he knew.

"If Boss ever finds out I've told you . . ." Enos finished up, giving a little shudder.

"Don't worry, your secret is safe with us," said Uncle Jesse, patting him on the back. "An' you did the right thing, boy. You sure did."

After Enos had gone the Dukes sat round the kitchen table discussing what they could do now. It was Daisy who came up with the answer.

"I've got it!" she said suddenly, snapping her fingers in delight. "Why didn't we think of it before? There's the annual best mechanic competition coming up soon. You

"We'll beat that cheatin' critter yet, and here's how . . ."

The plan worked? Well, of course it did!

Next morning Bo went round to Cooter's place to tell him what they'd found out, ending up: "... so Cooter, you just gotta enter that competition."

Cooter readily agreed, knowing that he could beat any mechanic in the county, probably even if he kept his eyes closed.

Boss took a bit more persuading, but with Enos to give them the inside information the boys eventually found out that Boss had agreed to enter the contest — but that he'd made some rather special plans ...

Contestants took their own cars to work on during the competition. One of the judges would disconnect various bits and pieces in the engine and the one who could put it all together again fastest was the winner. Enos told the boys that Boss was arranging to have a real terrific mechanic from out of state hide in the passenger seat and whisper the instructions to the sneaky Boss.

Luckily, Enos knew the mechanic personally, and when he explained to him what was going on the mechanic agreed to slip out of the car at the last minute — and let Bo climb in.

Come the competition ...

There was a tense atmosphere in the hall where the competition was being held. Quite a few mechanics had entered, but looking around Cooter knew that none of them were going to be able to beat him. Only Boss, believing that he had the paid mechanic hidden safely in the car, thought he'd show Cooter a thing or two.

"Let the competition ... Commence!"

At the judge's announcement several heads disappeared inside several hoods, as the audience began to shout encouragements to the competitors they wanted to win.

The noise didn't bother Cooter, who knew every bolt and every screw in every engine you care to mention.

But as for poor Boss . . . Well, it was hard enough trying to catch the whispered instructions from inside the car with all that row going on, and then there was the problem that what this guy was telling him didn't seem to be making any sense at all!

Boss didn't know much about cars, but he sure was confused when the voice told him to do things like: "Connect the carburettor to the silencer" and "Pull the outlet hose off the petrol tank".

"Are you *sure*?" Boss kept hissing, as the voice told him to do crazier and crazier sounding things. But he had to go along with it, and hope for the best.

"All competitors . . . Stop!"

The competition had come to an end and the judging was beginning. As expected Cooter's efforts received every praise and commendation the judges could heap on him. Then there was just one more entry to judge — Boss's car.

One judge peered inside the hood. He called over another judge: "Here, Deke — come an' get a look at this!"

"Good, eh?" smiled Boss, rather misinterpreting what was going on.

Soon all six of the judges were clustered round Boss's car, scratching their heads in amazement. "Mr Hogg," said one of them at last.

"Yessir?" answered Boss. "Do I take the first prize?"

"Not exactly," replied the judge. "You take the booby prize. In all my years of judging I have never seen an engine so badly put together. It's truly unbelievable."

Still trying, Rosco?

That ol' plan of the Dukes sure worked a treat . . .

Come the following morning, bright an' early, Luke an' Uncle Jesse were waiting outside Cooter's place to welcome him when he opened up again.

"You're back in business, Cooter!" said Uncle Jesse delightedly, as they heard Cooter's phone ringing with the first of many bookings for the day.

Matter of fact, Cooter was so busy that it wasn't until the following week that he was able to get on over to the hall where the competition had been held, and put Boss's engine together again. Poor old Boss just had to do without his precious car for a while — no way was it gonna start, not considering what Boss had done to it!

And anyway, before he fixed the Cadillac Cooter had another official vehicle to work on. Boss had instructed Rosco to bring in the Dukes on some trumped up charge or other, as he sure suspected they were behind that competition business.

Rosco had chased the General all over Hazzard County, and in doing so had busted a fender, broken a headlight, and worn out the clutch pedal.

All that was good business for Cooter.

And no, just in case you're wonderin', Rosco never did catch up with the Dukes . . .

Thrust 2. The Fastest Car on Earth

Photos by C. Noble. Copyright Thrust Cars Ltd.

The fastest car on earth. Thrust 2 is over 27 feet long and weighs 4 tons. The Rolls-Royce Avon jet engine develops 16,800 lbs thrust — equivalent to an astonishing 30,000 horsepower.

In 1977, when Richard Noble decided that he would try to recover the World Land Speed Record for Britain, he was in no doubt about the formidable difficulties he faced.

Britain had last held the record in 1964 when the late Donald Campbell reached 403 mph in his famous car 'Bluebird', at Lake Eyre, Australia. Since then the record had been held by the USA and had been pushed to an incredible 622 mph.

Richard Noble knew he would have to aim at reaching 650 mph.

He recalls that the time he had the following . . . no car, no experience, no workshop, no tools, no equipment, no team and no money!

What he did have was an engine. It was 22 years old — a Rolls-Royce Avon jet taken from a Lightning fighter — and its sterling performance was to prove a fitting tribute to British engineering skills.

'Project Thrust' went ahead.

A fine team of experts rallied to help Richard Noble. Their skills had to cover a multitude of specialist jobs, including chassis design, jet engines and electronics. As designer, John Ackroyd had overall responsibility for building the car, using components which could be maintained as cheaply as possible.

A number of manufacturers and commercial companies gave invaluable support to the team. They put up cash, or contributed components, or lent out skilled staff. Without the foresight and backing of these sponsors Project Thrust could not have succeeded.

Designer John Ackroyd was required to find answers to some rather disturbing questions. Where and when should they make the attempt? They would need a flat, firm track of at least 13 miles — and good weather. What kind of tyres can be relied upon at that speed? Solid metal wheels had to be specially designed. How do we stop a 4 ton car safely at 650 mph? Certainly not with the braking system of a family saloon. In fact, the first two stages of braking were by parachutes released behind Thrust 2, which reduced the speed until disc brakes could safely take over.

When asked how long the engine would withstand the appalling 'flat out' treatment it was receiving, John Watkins, an RAF expert, could only advise Richard Noble: "Put your foot down and think of England."

The choice of track was of paramount importance. Bonneville Flats in Utah, USA, had been a favourite venue, and in 1981 Richard Noble made his first attempt there — but it was 'flooded off'.

Thrust 2 flat out at 650 mph in the Black Rock Desert. From a standing start it covered 10½ miles in 110 seconds, and reached 650 mph in just 59 seconds. It used 10 gallons of fuel per mile!

Richard Noble and Thrust 2. World Record holders. October 1983.

The next attempt was delayed because of an accident whilst testing the car at an airbase in Britain. A braking fault sent Thrust 2 careering off the runway at almost 300 mph. Fortunately, although the car was badly damaged, Richard Noble and his passenger walked away from the wreckage unhurt. At least they had given the meticulous cockpit safety features a really thorough 'road test'!

Back at Bonneville, in September 1982, the team was again greeted by a flooded track. In despair they looked for an alternative site and found it in Nevada — the Black Rock Desert. Here, despite further delays and poor conditions, Thrust 2 set a new British record of 590 mph, but fell short of the World Record.

The team spent that winter preparing for a final attempt in 1983.

In September 1983 the team was back in the Black Rock Desert, determined to finish the task they had started in 1977. But things didn't look good. The weather and track were far from ideal.

First runs were over 600 mph, but still short of the record. Time was running out. The weather was likely to get worse, not better, and now there were problems with the car.

It was to be one final all-out effort. Modifications were made to the fuel system, the wheels and the suspension. They would make their final attempt at the hottest time of the day when drag is reduced and speed increases . . . but would the weather hold?

The morning of 4th October dawned clear and still. The temperature rose steadily, and at 3 pm they were all set to go but — unbelievably — the engine would not start. An igniter fuse had failed and a replacement had to be fitted.

Forty hectic minutes later the engine roared into life and Richard Noble was away to a blistering first run of 624 mph.

Quickly the team prepared for the second run. Thrust 2 shot away down the desert track reaching an incredible 650 mph in just 59 seconds, and recording almost 643 mph over the measured mile. The average of these two runs was 633.468 mph.

The record was theirs!

The skill, determination and courage of Richard Noble and his dedicated Project Thrust team, together with the performance of a 22-year-old Rolls-Royce aero engine, had achieved a spectacular goal.

Thrust 2 really was 'the fastest car on earth'.

By remarkable coincidence Richard Noble learned that in 1851 a prospector named William Noble had also travelled the Black Rock trail, pioneering a route to California. Whilst his namesake would have been pleased if his wagon train managed 10 miles a day, Richard Noble was planning to cover the same distance in less than two minutes!

Would you believe it!

It's hard to believe some of the crazy stunts the General gets up to in the course of the average week! Here are some more hard-to-believe facts about the world of motoring.

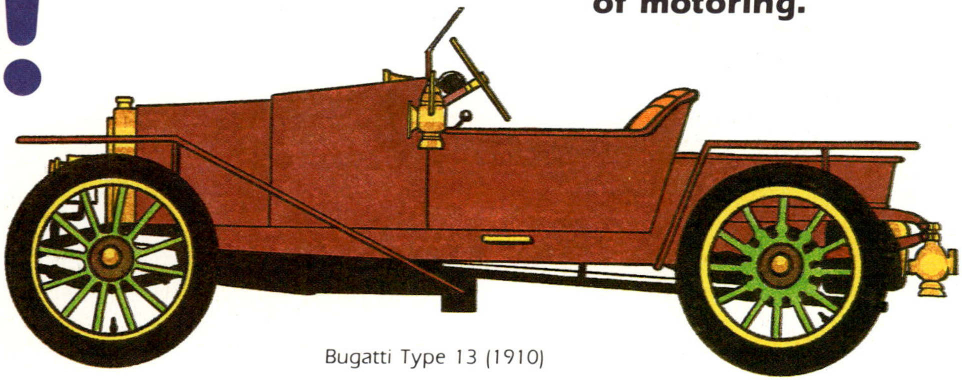

Bugatti Type 13 (1910)

Bugatti Type 57S

A Great Name

In over 30 years of motor car manufacture, the Bugatti factory turned out only 7,000 cars — yet their name is amongst the 'greats' in motoring. Bugatti cars were, in every respect, quite simply superb, and many are still in perfect running order, taking the pride of place in collections all over the world.

The Computer Chauffeur

Computers are taking over more and more functions of our everyday life, and if one new idea gets the go-ahead they might soon be driving our cars! The idea is for motorways to have inbuilt guidance pathways, consisting of cables buried beneath each lane, giving signals to the cars above. On joining the motorway the driver would slot a coded card into a machine at the side of the road. The card would tell the machine how far the driver wanted to go, and from there on the

Steam Car (1899)

computers would be in charge. Sitting back to enjoy his journey, the driver would be alerted when approaching the exit he required by a buzzer sound, and he would then resume control of the car.

The General Lee is a 1969 model Dodge Charger. He's quite a car!

Boss's white Cadillac is his pride and joy. Cadillac have long been one of America's leading car manufacturers, building their reputation in the early 1900s with luxurious, comfortable cars. Even in those early years, when motoring was inclined to be a noisy business, riding in a Cadillac was a smooth, silent sensation.

Early Days

In the early days of motoring, there were a number of intriguing devices intended to protect the vehicle against theft. One of the most bizarre was a 'collapsible rubber driver' — in other words, a blow-up figure which you sat in your driving seat whenever you left your car!

Accidents happened even at the very beginning of motoring history, and soon there were laws to ensure greater safety for pedestrians. Some drivers wore 'mouth sirens' on their wrists. These were whistles, intended to be used as well as the horn, to warn walkers of your approach. In actual fact, though, the noise of the engine was so great that often neither horn nor siren could be heard above it!

Saved

Uncle Jesse had a feeling it was gonna be 'one of those days' right from the moment he climbed out of bed that morning. Amazin' how right these country folks can be sometimes . . .

Uncle Jesse heard the sounds of whispering voices and scurrying footsteps only seconds before the two guys pounced. He didn't have a moment to defend himself against them when they ran up behind him, grabbed him forcibly by an arm each, and dragged him over to a chair by the porch.

"Gotcha, old timer!" hissed one of the intruders, and the other one laughed. Then the two of them set about tying up Uncle Jesse with rope, and using his own neckerchief to stop him calling for help.

"What's going on here . . ." was the last thing Uncle Jesse was able to say, before they gagged him, and left him stranded there, by the porch.

The two guys immediately made a run for their car, and Uncle Jesse just managed to catch the plates as they skidded away at top speed. He kept repeating the figures over and over again in his head as he sat there, unable to figure what on earth could be going on.

The two young men hadn't stolen anything from out of the house, he was sure of that. And they hadn't done any damage either. So why in Hazzard did they want to go tying up people?

Then another thought struck Uncle Jesse. The boys were already out for the day, and Daisy had gone on over to a neighbour's place to look after three kiddies whilst their ma went into town.

"I could be here for hours," he thought, as he shifted uncomfortably in the seat.

But Uncle Jesse had reckoned without old Mr Snow White. That was the name the family gave their white cockerel, and he had a favourite perch right by where Uncle Jesse was tied up.

Luckily enough, he had decided to spend some time on that particular perch that morning, and soon as he came walking through the yard, Uncle Jesse knew that the big bird might be able to help him.

Mr Snow White could see there was something up at once. He wasn't exactly the brightest of birds, but then again he knew pretty well that this old hillbilly, who came each night and morning to give him corn, didn't usually sit there in a chair with

by the Bird

The scene of the crime.

ropes round him!

Mr Snow White decided on the only course of action open to him. He hollered, and he hollered, and he hollered . . . Cock-a-doodle-dooo . . .!

Over at the neighbour's place, Daisy heard a familiar sound. Why was Mr Snow White kicking up such a fuss? Daisy decided she'd better go find out . . .

The three children Daisy was looking after thought it was very exciting to be going round rescuing tied-up neighbours, but poor Daisy was frantic with worry as she set Uncle Jesse free. Would he be all right?

Uncle Jesse seemed none the worse for wear as he rubbed his arms where the ropes had been tight, and he quickly gave Daisy the plates of the car the men had been driving.

Daisy went off to CB the boys and Rosco with the news, whilst Uncle Jesse and the neighbour's children heaped praise upon old Mr Snow White.

Bo 'n' Luke and Rosco were astonished at what they heard

"O.K. Hold it right there!"

from Daisy over the CB, and they all dropped what they were doing immediately and set off to track down the car.

It was the General who found it first, and as the occupants were taken completely by surprise the boys were easily able to overtake and force them to stop.

As you can imagine they weren't too friendly to the guys who had manhandled Uncle Jesse, but they decided it was best to let the law deal with them, and they drove them straight into town, where Enos immediately locked them in the cells.

The Dukes went off home then, to check out for themselves that Uncle Jesse really was OK, and it was left to Enos to interrogate the men, and find out just what they were up to.

Over dinner that evening . . .

"... so it was all a stunt to raise runds for charity," finished up Bo, who had just come off the phone after talking to Enos. He'd told the family everything Enos had told him: about how the young guys were students from a university out of state, having one of those crazy weeks when they all get up to stunts to make money for good causes.

"But I don't understand,"

"I've bin thinkin', Daisy . . ."

said Daisy. "How were they going to make any money out of tying up Uncle Jesse?"

"Seems they were planning to run a protection racket," said Bo, shaking his head at the mad idea. "They were gonna contact us, and say that if we didn't want it to happen again we'd have to pay them twenty dollars."

"Huh," said Luke, disgusted, "all that worry and discomfort for Uncle Jesse, and all to make twenty dollars. Gee, those crazy guys. They deserve whatever punishment they got coming to them."

Bo nodded emphatically, and they continued with their meal, glad that Uncle Jesse seemed quite recovered from his ordeal by now.

He was rather quiet though, and he remained very thoughtful throughout the meal. Later on, when he and Daisy took a stroll round the farm in the evening cool, he told her what was on his mind.

"I've been thinkin', Daisy," he began. "Those guys acted pretty crazy, that's for sure; but young people often do hot-headed things, and regret it real bad afterwards. An' they were doing it all for charity."

"But, they tied you up . . ." interrupted Daisy.

"Yeah, but they didn't hurt me none," smiled Uncle Jesse. "I reckon as how they'll feel pretty bad about things after a night in Rosco's cells. I wouldn't like to think of them being punished any more."

"But, Uncle Jesse . . ." protested Daisy.

Weren't no way Daisy was gonna change Uncle Jesse's mind, though she sure tried hard. The boys too, when they heard what he was planning to do. But when Uncle Jesse's mind's made up, Uncle Jesse's mind's made up . . .

". . . so I want you to be lenient with those guys, Boss," Uncle Jesse finished up. "And I don't want to press charges."

It was the following morning, and Uncle Jesse had gone straight on into town to plead with Boss to let the two young men off with a warning.

He had a hard job convincing Boss to agree, but finally he managed it, and Boss promised that he wouldn't impose a fine

"Just this once, Jesse."

"Sittin' here in court makes me a mite uncomfortable!"

thinking about all the jobs there were to do around the place!

But something was still bothering the students.

"We promised to raise some cash for charity," said one of them.

"Yeah," said the other. "How're we gonna do it now?"

Know how much the General likes stunts? And 'specially when it's all in a good cause . . .

Yep, that's right. Bo 'n' Luke volunteered to put on a show of stunts in the General, and sell tickets to raise money for the

or a jail sentence. "But I'm gonna make them sweat it out in court," he added, with a gleeful grin.

Bo and Luke still didn't really agree with what Uncle Jesse had done, but they stood by his decision of course, and even went along to the court case to make sure that Boss kept his word.

Well, he did — both parts of it. He finally let the young students off with a warning — but he gave them such a rough time in court that they'd really had plenty of punishment by the time they came out.

That, coupled with the opportunity they'd had the previous night for some long, hard thinking, had really shown them the errors of their ways, and they realised now what a stupid thing they had done.

They were full of remorse as they stood talking to the Duke boys later on, outside the court, and when they heard how it had been Uncle Jesse who'd pleaded to get them let off, they felt even worse! They volunteered to do two days' work around the farm, to make amends.

"You're on," smiled Luke,

The magnificent motor in action.

charity.

The event turned out to be a big success; all three of them — that is, Bo, Luke, and the General — enjoyed themselves tremendously — and all in a good cause.

Come the following Saturday brunchtime, Boss was invited on over to the Dukes' place . . .

Daisy cooked a delicious brunch for them all, with Boss as their honoured guest, to thank him for letting the boys off with a warning, as Uncle Jesse had asked.

"Looks like I've bin good for once, huh?"

Boss had obviously been giving the whole matter some serious thought, because when all the things were cleared away he posed a question which had been on his mind throughout the meal.

"Jesse," he began, "one thing puzzles me."

"Yeah, Boss, what's that?" asked Jesse.

'What did I get out of it all?" was the question.

"Why, Boss, you got the satisfaction of having done a good deed," replied Uncle Jesse readily.

"Oh, so that's what I got, is it?" said Boss, pondering the idea. "Satisfaction, eh? Good deed, you say? Aha . . . Hmmmm."

Ten Tricky Teasers

1. Enos is Deputy Sheriff of Hazzard County. Who plays the part of Enos?

2. It was midnight on the third Sunday in the month, and raining heavily. Uncle Jesse looked out of the window and predicted: "In 72 hours' time it still won't be sunny." How could he be so sure?

3. There is three errers in this sentence. Can you find them?

4. What is the name of the actor who plays Uncle Jesse?

5. Is it legal in Hazzard for a man to marry his widow's sister?

6. Two men were playing checkers. They played 5 games each, and each won the same number. How come?

7. Bo put a dollar bill in an empty bottle, then corked it firmly. How could he get his money out again without pulling the cork or breaking the bottle?

8. An electric train was going through Hazzard County in a north-easterly direction. The wind was blowing south-westerly. Which way would the engine smoke be blowing?

9. Take a good look at this picture of the Boar's Nest, then close the book, and see how many of the different bits and pieces you can remember. Write them down and then compare your list with the picture. Challenge a friend to remember more.

Answers

1. Sonny Shroyer.
2. In 72 hours' time it would be midnight again, so it certainly wouldn't be sunny.
3. The first two should be obvious. The third is that there are only two errors!
4. Denver Pyle.
5. A man who has a **widow** isn't in a position to marry anyone else!
6. They weren't playing each other.
7. Bo could push the cork into the bottle.
8. Electric trains don't have engine smoke.
9. Well, how did you do?

Daisy's Terrific Truffles

Daisy served up these truly terrific truffles at a Hallowe'en party given by the Dukes last year — an' they sure went down a treat.

Why don't y'all try them, too?

You'll need:

For the truffles:
225 g (8 oz) sponge cake crumbs
50 g (2 oz) walnuts, toasted hazelnuts or almonds, finely chopped
3 tablespoons cocoa powder
4 tablespoons set honey
1–2 tablespoons orange juice

For the coating:
cocoa powder
or
drinking chocolate
or
desiccated coconut

(This amount of mixture makes 24 truffles)

Method:
1. Put all the ingredients together in a large mixing bowl.
2. Work everything together until you have a firm, even mixture. (You might find it easiest to start with a wooden spoon, then use your hands as the mixture becomes firmer. Make sure they're clean first.)
3. Divide the mixture into four.
4. Out of each section of mixture make 6 small balls, rolling them in your hands till they are nicely rounded.
5. Roll the balls in your chosen coating.
6. Chill in the fridge for a few hours before eating.

P.S. These truffles are delicious made with 1–2 tablespoons of dark rum instead of the orange juice, if you're allowed to use it.

Butting In

Ever had a goat around the place? They sure do make tricky house pets . . .

". . . an' then when he'd finished chewin' my new boots he started on the new auto magazine I'd just bought in town. We're gonna have to do something."

Bo finished telling Luke all the latest catalogue of mischief which the family's pet goat had been up to that week. As usual, he had wreaked havoc with someone's possessions, and this time it seemed as though they'd all been Bo's things.

"Don't look at me," replied Luke. "I'm the one who volunteered to take him to those obedience classes."

"But they were for dogs," countered Bo.

"I know that," insisted Luke, "but the lady who ran them reckoned she was such a whizz with animals she could tame anything from a lion to a limpet."

"She was wrong then, wasn't she?" commented Bo.

"Yeah well, she'd have gotten on a lot better if she'd used her copy of 'How To Tame All Sorts of Animals'," said Luke, coming to the trainer's defence.

"And why didn't she use it?" persisted Bo.

"Our goat had eaten it by the

"It ain't easy training a goat, you know . . ."

time she arrived for class," replied Luke. "An' then there was the business over her packed lunch . . ."

"No wonder you were asked to leave," said Bo, grinning.

Just then their conversation was interrupted by the arrival of Daisy, who came to tell them they had a visitor.

Talk about surprise guests . . .

The visitor was none other than Boss J. D. Hogg, who, as Daisy told the boys, was apparently just paying them a pleasant social call to see how they were all keeping. He planned to stay a while, and take some happy snapshots of the Duke family.

"Something fishy going on here," said Bo.

"Yeah, that's what I figured," replied Daisy. "That's why I came on out here to get you guys. Uncle Jesse says everyone has some kindliness and we gotta give him the benefit of the doubt, but . . ."

"I agree with you, Daisy," nodded Luke, anticipating what Daisy was about to say. All three of them knew pretty well that where the milk of human kindness was concerned, Boss's bottle only parted with a few drops round about once in a blue moon!

"Something fishy going on," repeated Bo.

The three Dukes reckoned Boss's visit needed a little more lookin' into, and they all went on inside to check it out . . .

They found Boss and Uncle Jesse settled down over a pot of coffee and some of Daisy's home made chocolate cookies, apparently getting on like old buddies. Boss seemed to be in a right neighbourly mood, and soon all the Dukes were beginning to wonder if they'd misjudged him all these years.

Perhaps he was a real good guy at heart?

"Well gee, I've had such a good time out here this afternoon," said Boss at last.

"Boys, this ain't no ordinary housecall!"

"Say CHEESE!"

"Reckon I'd like to have a memento of our happy time together. Let's all go out in the yard an' I'll take some snapshots."

The Dukes were still a bit puzzled about this change of heart, but they went along with Boss's suggestion, smartened themselves up, and went into the yard to pose for the photos.

Boss took quite a few shots of them all, until he seemed satisfied that he had what he wanted.

"Just one more, you guys," he said at last, peering through the viewfinder of his camera and checking that the light was OK.

Now, if Boss hadn't taken that one last photo, the end of this story might have been quite different. As you'll see, it was lucky he did . . .

"Daisy, move to the left a fraction," Boss was saying, apparently not quite happy with the way they were all posing. "Uncle Jesse, just take one step to the right . . ."

And then it happened. That old goat of theirs seemingly decided to take a closer look at the photograph-taking proceedings, and came closer to check things out. What he found was someone with some mighty interesting-looking back pockets bending down just in front of him. And he sure was hungry, having had nothing but a short piece of washing line to eat since breakfast . . .

"Look out, Boss!" cried Daisy, who was the first to notice. But it was too late.

"Just one step to the right, Jesse."

Mmm, looks like mealtime's come around again . . .

With just one nip of his sharp teeth the goat was into Boss's pocket, and immediately had the contents all strewn about on the ground. Not finding anything particularly appetising there he turned his attention to the camera, and Boss retreated at speed.

The goat wasn't put off that easily though, and there began a high-speed chase round the yard, with Boss running as fast as he could and the goat running faster. Soon it wasn't quite clear who was chasing whom, and undoubtedly the goat by now thought it was all some new sort of game. But Boss clearly wasn't finding it that entertaining!

While all that was going on, the Dukes rushed over to pick up Boss's belongings, and try to dust them off a bit.

But what they found was what you might call an eye-opener . . .

"What's this?" said Daisy, holding up a photograph of an illicit moonshine still. "Why's he carrying this around?"

"Put it back in Boss's wallet, Daisy," said Uncle Jesse. "It don't do to look at folks' personal things."

"You're right, Uncle Jesse," said Bo, holding a newspaper cutting in his hand. "In the ordinary way, that is. But ol' Boss sure ain't ordinary. Take a look at this."

Uncle Jesse started to read the newspaper cutting, and Luke and Daisy craned forward to read it over his shoulder. Moments later, light was dawning on all three faces.

"Says here that landowners who find out there's illegal goings-on on their property have the right to foreclose on their mortgages, and run their tenants off their land. That's if they have proof." Uncle Jesse finished the article and grinned.

All four Dukes ended up grinning as Bo summed up the whole thing:

"Landowners, that's Boss. Tenants, that's us. Illegal goings-on, that's an illicit still. Proof, that's photos."

"He was planning to take photos of us on his property, superimpose those shots of moonshine stills, and use the results as proof to foreclose on our mortgage," finished off Luke.

"To try to run us out of Hazzard," added Daisy.

Talking of running . . .

The four Dukes turned towards their gate, where the goat had just despatched Boss off their property. From the speed he was going, it looked like he was plannin' to run all the way back to town.

"Special treat for your supper tonight, old timer," said Uncle Jesse to the goat when it returned. "I'll see if I can find you a nice tasty book, or somethin' like that."

The goat looked pleased as he surveyed all their smiling faces. It was funny, he usually got into big trouble for escapades like this one. But you never could tell with humans . . .

It was left to Bo to have the last word: "Ain't no one gonna run us Dukes out of Hazzard, no sirree! The Dukes are here to stay!"

"See y'all!"